W9-BSN-375

Victims of the Latest Dance Craze
is the 1985
Lamont Poetry Selection of the
Academy of American Poets.

From 1954 through 1974 the Lamont
Poetry Selection supported the
publication and distribution of
twenty first books of poems. Since
1975 this distinguished award has
been given for an American poet's
second book.

Judges for 1985: Philip Booth,
Louise Glück and Charles Simic.

OMMATION PRESS
DIALOGUES ON DANCE SERIES

Linda M. Wagner, *Songs for Isadora,* #1
Karren LaLonde Alenier, *The Dancer's Muse,* #2
Ian Krieger, *Pavans,* #3
Liz LeBlanc, *No Mean Feet,* #4
Cornelius Eady, *Victims of the Latest Dance Craze,* #5

Dialogues on Dance number five

VICTIMS OF THE LATEST DANCE CRAZE

POEMS BY CORNELIUS EADY

ILLUSTRATIONS BY SUSAN MICKLEM

OMMATION PRESS 1986

This book is for Sarah Micklem

Published by Ommation Press, 5548 North Sawyer Avenue
Chicago, Illinois 60625

Copyright © 1985 by Cornelius Eady
First Edition
All Rights Reserved

ISBN 0-941240-02-9

Library of Congress Cataloging-in-Publication Data
Eady, Cornelius, 1954-
Victims of the latest dance craze.

(Dialogues on dance ; no. 5)
1. Dancing — Poetry. I. Title. II. Series:
Dialogues on dance ; # 5.
PS3555.A35V53 1986 811'.54 86-4311
ISBN 0-941240-02-9

Some of these poems appeared, at times in different versions,
in the following magazines:

Callaloo: "January"
New Letters: "The Dance"
Poet Lore: "Miss Johnson Dances for the First Time"
Poetry Now: "Radio", "The Robots"
Salome: "Dance Poem"
The Greenfield Review: "Aerial Ballet", "My Mother, If She Had Won Free Dance Lessons", "November"

"The Good Look", and "Victims of the Latest Dance Craze" first
appeared in *From Mt. San Angelo,* an anthology printed under
the auspices of Associated University Presses for the Virginia Center
for the Creative Arts.

Excerpt from "A Negro Love Song" by Paul Laurence Dunbar.
Reprinted with permission of Dodd, Mead and Company from
The Complete Poems of Paul Laurence Dunbar © by Dodd, Mead and Company.

I would like to thank the National Endowment for the Arts for their
support in the completion of this book.

Design and typography by The Design Group, Lynchburg, Virginia.
Cover Photographs © 1986 by David I. Abrams

TABLE OF CONTENTS

"Put my ahm aroun' huh wais',
  Jump back, honey, jump back.
Raised huh lips an' took a tase,
  Jump back, honey, jump back.
Love me, honey, love me true?
Love me well ez I love you?
An' she answe'd, " 'Cose I do"-
  Jump back, honey, jump back."

Paul Laurence Dunbar
"A Negro Love Song"

VICTIMS
OF THE LATEST
DANCE CRAZE

VICTIMS OF THE LATEST DANCE CRAZE

The streamers choking the main arteries
Of downtown.
The brass band led by a child
From the home for the handicapped.
The old men
Showing their hair (what's left of it),
The buttons of their shirts
Popping in time
To the salsa flooding out
Of their portable headphones,

And mothers letting their babies
Be held by strangers.
And the bus drivers
Taping over their fare boxes
And willing to give directions.

Is there any reason to mention
All the drinks are on the house?
Thick, adolescent boys
Dismantle their BB guns.

Here is the world (what's left of it),
In brilliant motion,
The oil slick at the curb
Danced into a thousand
Splintered steps.
The bag ladies toss off their
Garments
To reveal wings.

"This dance you do," drawls the cop,
"What do you call it?"
We call it scalding the air.
We call it dying with your
Shoes on.

And across the street
The bodies of tramps
Stumble
In a sober language.

And across the street
Shy young girls step behind
Their nameless boyfriends,
Twirling their skirts.

And under an archway
A delivery boy discovers
His body has learned to speak,
And what does this street look like
If not a runway,
A polished wood floor?

From the air,
Insects drawn by the sweat
Alight, when possible,
On the blur
Of torsos.
It is the ride
Of their tiny lives.

The wind that burns their wings,
The heaving, oblivious flesh,
Mountains stuffed with panic,
An ocean
That can't make up its mind.
They drop away
With the scorched taste
Of vertigo.

And under a swinging light bulb
Some children
Invent a game
With the shadow the bulb makes,
And the beat of their hearts.
They call it dust in the mouth.
They call it horse with no rider.
They call it school with empty books.

In the next room
Their mother throws her dress away to chance.
It drops to the floor
Like a brush sighs across a drum head,
And when she takes her lover,
What are they thinking of
If not a ballroom filled with mirrors,
A world where no one has the right
To stumble?

In a parking lot
An old man says this:
"I am a ghost dance.
I remember the way my hair felt,
Damp with sweat and wind.

When the wind kisses the leaves, I am dancing.
When the subway hits the third rail, I am dancing.
When the barrel goes over Niagara Falls, I am dancing.
Music rings my bones like metal.

MISS JOHNSON DANCES FOR THE FIRST TIME

When Ophelia met the water
It was a gentle tumble of a dance,
A mixed marriage of a dance.
The swans were confused.
She was a contradiction in terms.
She was, simply put, a beautiful death.

Not so with Miss Johnson,
A wheat field of a girl,
Who held her breath
As she cast herself on the dance floor
In a metallic blue dress

At the Grange Hall on Saturday night,
Holding onto a skinny mechanic

Who knew two steps
That could be shown in public.

It was like being pushed off the raft by her father:
The awful moment when the body believes in nothing.
How ridiculous her body looked,

How her brothers loved to remind her:
A wharf rat.
A drowned cow.

When Amelia Earhart met the water,
Assuming, of course, that she met the water,
Did the sea mistake her for a bird
Or flying fish?

In the awkward moment she belonged neither to sea
  nor air,
Did she move like Miss Johnson moves now,
Bobbing like a buoy at high tide,
Gulping mouthfuls of air
As her legs learn the beat and push,
And her blue dress catches the mechanic's pant leg
Like an undertow?

THE DANCE OF EVE

Eve,
Her mind now filled with
The red, voluptuous curve
  of the apples,
Glances over at her husband
On what we will call Friday night.

We can only imagine the night sky,
The fresh stars burning in the clear air,
The symphony of insects, the lost cries
  of animals whose contracts
God will, to put it gently,
Decide not to pick up on option.
Eve glances over at her husband
With a pang she can only name
  as not hunger.

As Adam sits there, weeds and the dry
  husks of insects
In a semi-circle at his feet,
His tongue dry with names,
The joints of his shoulders sore
  from the lifting and asking,

Eve walks towards him,
Apple extended in her hand,
Neither one quite sure of what
Her body is trying to promise.

APRIL

Suddenly, the legs want a different sort of work.
This is because the eyes look out the window
And the sight is filled with hope.
This is because the eyes look out the window

And the street looks a fraction better than
  the day before.
This is what the eyes tell the legs,
Whose joints become smeared with a fresh sap
Which would bud if attached to a different limb.

The legs want a different sort of work.
This is because the ears hear what they've been
  waiting for,
Which cannot be described in words,
But makes the heart beat faster, as if
One had just found money in the street.

The legs want to put on a show for the entire world.
The legs want to reclaim their gracefulness.
This is because the nose at last finds the right scent
And tugs the protesting body onto the dance floor.
This is because the hands, stretching out in boredom,
Accidentally brush against the skirts of the world.

AERIAL BALLET

I am not done with my falling.
I turn in the air like a fish,
Who realizes he is a fish
Somehow in the middle
Of a tragic miracle.
Do you wish to know about the tiny stars?
Very well,
I will tell you about the tiny stars.
I am a tiny star.
My fingers burn in the air

Leaving a vapor trail
That might be mistaken for a jet.

I am not done with my falling.
I turn in the air like a rock
That has always dreamed of being
A great, weightless contradiction.
New York at dusk
Is a cluster of tiny, grounded stars,
And as I burn towards their heart
A great peace lightens my bones.

I am not done with my falling.
I turn in the air like a snake
Dreaming off a bad meal.
I am dropped from a bird
Beneath a canopy of stars
Which hiss like the campfires I fall towards
That will make who knows what out of
This awkward story.

I am not done with my falling.
I am following my blood,
Which has decided to court the streets of New York
in its own strange fashion.
I see the moon,
A pale specter of a star,
Softly appear like smoke before a fire,
And as I plunge, the streets forever curl away
Like cellophane beneath a match.

THE GOOD LOOK

It is like my father,
His legs turning to rubber,
Taking what he believes to be
His last look at our house.
I imagine my mother, his
Crazy wife,
Standing at the front door,
Believing it all an elaborate stunt,
Or peeking through
The living room blinds
Making as small a target
As possible.

He breathes.
The street reels under his feet,
And now he is like an intoxicated dancer,
Luck wheezing out of his mouth,
Propped up by cousins
Leading him to the open maw
Of their car door

Which becomes
The line that marks
The borders of the world as
  he knows it,
The line which, once crossed,
Is forever denied.

My father
Stops at that portal,
And, though totally mistaken,
Takes a hard look at his house.

Everything the words *so long* were ever
Meant to imply
Is in this look,
A look that, when shown to me later,
Second-hand,
As part of a story with a
Happy ending,

Nevertheless
Raises the ante.

JOHNNY LACES UP HIS RED SHOES

If Fred Astaire had been really smart,
He would have danced like Johnny dances on Friday night,
With his brilliant red shoes
That women can detect half a block away.

If Fred Astaire had been all he was cracked up to be,
He would have danced like Johnny dances on Friday night,
On two pools of quicksilver
Painted fire-engine red.

Johnny is lacing up his red shoes.
He is a pizza,
A kiss in the dark.
And as his fingers tie the laces,
He thinks of long, dark hair.

On his bitter-sweet sofa bed
Johnny is lacing up his red shoes,
And as his fingers tighten the laces,
His work clothes slide deeper
Into the evening shadows.

If Fred Astaire had been serious,
He would have walked through the door of the neighborhood bar
  like Johnny does on Friday night,
Wearing two small volcanos
That are permitted to erupt for only three nights.

DANCE POEM

People who want to be dancers
Should know the rules:
Learn to love yourself.
Be ready for failure.

Don't have poets for friends.
They love to eat.
They're a constant temptation.
On top of that,
They will try
To put a dance
Of life
Onto paper,
And demand that you understand it.

You will need medicine:
Powders for your feet,
Salve for tired muscles,
And maybe,
At times,
When your art permits,
Someone to rub it on.

POET DANCES WITH INANIMATE OBJECT

for Jim Schley

The umbrella, in this case;
Earlier, the stool, the
Wooden pillars that hold up
  the roof.

This guy, you realize,
Will dance with anything —
— He likes the idea.

Then he picks up some lady's discarded sandals,
Holds them next to his head like sea shells,
Donkey ears.

Nothing,
    his body states,
Is safe from the dance of ideas!

RADIO

There is the woman
Who will not listen
To music. There is the man
Who dreams of kissing the lips
Attached to the voice.
There is the singer
Who reinvents the world
In musical notation.
There is the young couple
Who dance slowly on the sidewalk,
As if the rest of the street
Didn't exist.
There is the school boy
Whose one possession
Is an electric box
That scrambles the neighborhood.
There is the young girl
Who locks her bedroom door,
And lip-syncs in the mirror.
There is the young beau
Who believes in the songs so much,
He hears them
Even when
He isn't kissing someone.
There is the mother
Who absent-mindedly sways to the beat,
But fears the implications
For her daughter.
There is the man
Who carries one in his
Breast pocket,
And pretends it's a Luger.

There are the two young punks
Who lug one into our car
On the stalled D train,
Who, as we tense for the assault,
Tune in a classical music station,
As if this were Saturday night
On another world.

NOVEMBER

Everything fails.
God damn this cold
And this static electricity.
Like the leaves,
I have given up.
Words have become a jelly-like substance
At the base of the skull.

It is another thing I haven't
Asked for.
I take what I get,
And what I've got

Is a lawn filled with surrender,
Snakeskins,
Shipwrecks,

A porch littered with consequence
And scientific fact.

This is the gravity dance.
The same thing that draws us together
Has ruined all these dresses.

THE LOST POEM

for Owen Andrews

A young poet sees a sunset.
There is something about it,
 the color of it,
Plus

A scrap of conversation
At the end:
"No," I believe he says to somebody there,
"It's not a sunset."

All year, his friend explains to me,
He writes the poem
And misses the point.
The point is,

The poem is really about confusion,
Like walking up to the back of a dress
At a dance and having it turn,
A stranger,

Not the person who walked in on
 your arm.
The poem is really about

The man, drawing back,
His smile evaporating into
 good manners,

His eyes scanning the room
 for landmarks,
Not quite certain now
Where he is,

The indescribable smirk that blossoms
  on the girl's face
As she walks away,
Leaving him to hold the bones
Of this moment,
So strange, so ethereal,

Nothing
Will ever blink it back.

MY MOTHER, IF SHE HAD WON FREE DANCE LESSONS

Would she have been a person
With a completely different outlook on life?
There are times when I visit
And find her settled on a chair
In our dilapidated house,
The neighborhood crazy lady
Doing what the neighborhood crazy lady is
  supposed to do,
Which is absolutely nothing

And I wonder as we talk our sympathetic talk,
Abandoned in easy dialogue,
I, the son of the crazy lady,
Who crosses easily into her point of view
As if yawning
Or taking off an overcoat.
Each time I visit
I walk back into our lives

And I wonder, like any child who wakes up one day
  to find themself
Abandoned in a world larger than their
  Bad dreams,
I wonder as I see my mother sitting there,
Landed to the right-hand window in the living room,
Pausing from time to time in the endless loop
  of our dialogue
To peek for rascals through the
Venetian blinds,

I wonder a small thought.
I walk back into our lives.
Given the opportunity,
How would she have danced?
Would it have been as easily

As we talk to each other now,
The crazy lady
And the crazy lady's son,
As if we were old friends from opposite coasts
Picking up the thread of a long conversation,

Or two ballroom dancers
Who only know
One step?

What would have changed
If the phone had rung like a suitor,
If the invitation had arrived in the mail
Like Jesus, extending a hand?

THE POETIC INTERPRETATION OF THE TWIST

I know what you're expecting to hear.
You think to yourself: Here's a guy who must understand what
  the twist was all about.
Look at the knuckles of his hands,
Look at his plain, blue shirt hanging out of the back
  of his trousers.
The twist must have been the equivalent of
  the high sign
In a secret cult.

I know
I know
I know

But listen: I am still confused by the mini-skirt
As well as the deep meaning of vinyl on everything.
The twist was just a children's game to us.
I know you expect there ought to be more to this,
The reason the whole world decided to uncouple,

But why should I lie to you? Let me pull up a chair
And in as few words as possible,
Re-create my sister,
Who was renowned for running like a giraffe.
Let me re-create my neighborhood,
A dead-end street next to the railroad tracks.
Let me re-create
My father, who would escape the house by bicycle
And do all the grocery shopping by himself.

Let's not forget the pool hall and the barbershop,
Each with their strange flavors of men,
And while we're on the subject,
I must not slight the ragweed,
The true rose of the street.

All this will still not give you the twist.

Forgive me for running on like this.
Your question has set an expectation
That is impossible to meet

Your question has put on my shoulders
A troublesome responsibility

Because the twist is gone.
It is the foundation of a bridge
That has made way for a housing project

And I am sorry to admit
You have come to the wrong person.
I recall the twist
The way we recall meeting a distant aunt as a baby
Or the afternoons spent in homeroom
Waiting for the last bell.

My head hurts.
I am tired of remembering.
Perhaps you can refresh my memory
And tell me
How we got on this topic?
As a favor to me,
Let's not talk anymore about old dances.

I have an entire world on the tip of my tongue.

PIANO CONCERT

for Carol Rhodes

What I have always wanted
And all I have always wanted
Is to know an object this perfectly,
To hear my body ring against it,

To keep a piece of this afternoon's light
With its blot of notes
Like sugar on my tongue.

Is that asking too much?
What I see in your hands
As they wing over the keyboard
Seeps into my bones, lightens me.

I'm not so young that I believe
This will do me any good,
This longing my legs have to bounce
This way,

But I am tired of my eyes glazing
When I read,
The sick light that seems to fall
Over everything. What I want now

Is a sustained chord in my belly,
The uncoiling of the secret
Deep within my muscles. What I want now
Is to rise with these notes

And keep rising.

CHOREOGRAPHING YOUR NEW HOUSE

for Kathy Lance and Albert Fink

You were trying to find an answer to the
question posed by the exposed studs
in your walls. I remember us

Trying to do the neighborly thing. The living room
blossomed like a lawn filmed with a
high speed camera, drapes and rugs flowered and
died each time one of you changed
your mind. I remember thinking of a waltz
as your eyes diagrammed

The floor. We couldn't feel the motion, but I
knew we were being unpacked, we
danced with your sofas and chairs,
we

Spun in time, you dressed us in
formal gowns and sweat shirts, we

Held beer cans and champagne glasses, we
laughed in our party voices and spoke
confidentially. You were choreographing
the empty room, showing us the chalk marks.
We tried to do the neighborly thing.

We let you lead.

JANUARY

The old man wants to dance
But can't get started.
May I dance with you? Not yet,
Laughs the beautiful girl
As she spins away
In an air-light
Dress.

He'll never catch up.
It's written right here in the script.
It has something to do
With the balance of the world.

If he catches her,
What will he lose?
The general feeling
That some ideals
Are impossible to live with.

But it will go harder on us.
It will be another thing
We can't just quite put our fingers on,
A slight feeling
Of uneasiness,

Something about the color of the sky,
An alien texture to the air.

The old man wants to dance.
Here are the hard facts:
She'll always be
A few steps ahead of him.

Not yet, she laughs.
Pursuing her,
The other months bounce along behind
Like cans
Tied to the honeymoon bumper.

THE ROBOTS

It is beautiful
To watch the robots
Take their baby steps
On the grass.

Nothing will be the same.
It is a story
That has been long
Overdue.

Some of my shift
Sit on the grass,
Others in the company bleachers.
A few have declared this event
A holiday
And are dressed
In beautiful, iridescent vests.

And now our supervisor,
A gruff man
With hands the angels might envy,
Wipes them on
His tattered, blue workshirt.

"Hey," he practically sings into
A reporter's lens,
"Who's going to trim
Your bonny hedges now?
Not us, buddy,
Not us, anymore,"
As he joy-sticks the machines
Past the local priest
Who sprinkles them
With holy water,
The boys from the Sr. High School Band
Making the most of

The opportunity,
One eye peeled for
Rumors,
The other for a girl
To expose them to.

And then they walk,
A Svengali Cabaret,
Pushing our mowers
Before them.

We cheer this blind date,
The perfect swathe
Behind their
Labor,
With all our hearts.

Our voices
Crack with leisure.

From the stands, through binoculars
I catch these details:
A single cloud
Passes over
A mirrored back,
A silver hand...

JACK JOHNSON DOES THE EAGLE ROCK

Perhaps he left the newspaper stand that morning
  dazed, a few pennies lighter,
The illustration of the crippled ocean liner
  with the berth he had the money
But not the skin to buy
Engraving itself
On that portion of the mind reserved for
  lucky breaks.
Perhaps the newsboy, a figure too small to
  bring back,
Actually heard his laugh,
As the *S.S. Titanic,* sans one prize fighter,
Goes down again all over New York,
Watched his body dance
As his arms lift the ship, now a simple millimeter thick,
  above his head
In the bustling air, lift it up
As though it was meant to happen.

WAFFLE HOUSE GIRL

Not much to this story: just a thin
  waitress, a southern girl at an
All-night diner. In fact,

She was slow with our orders, jumbled
The items the way you'd blow a good punchline.
The story was her nails,

Purple against the tan countertop, the
Shock of that color that late at night.
Two nights later, that detail scraped off
By whatever made her take the night shift,
Our orders served as if we weren't the only ones
Sitting in the booth,
I let go of my story of her dancing at the
  imagined go-go bar, the

Evening becoming a little stiff around the edges as I saw
  once again what I did not care to see.

THE EMPTY DANCE SHOES

My friends,
As it has been proven in the laboratory,
An empty pair of dance shoes
Will sit on the floor like a wart
Until it is given a reason to move.

Those of us who study inertia
(Those of us covered with wild hair and sleep)
Can state this without fear:
The energy in a pair of shoes at rest
Is about the same as that of a clown

Knocked flat by a sandbag.
This you can tell your friends with certainty:
A clown, flat on his back,
Is a lot like an empty pair of
  dancing shoes.

An empty pair of dancing shoes
Is also a lot like a leaf
Pressed in a book.
And now you know a simple truth:
A leaf pressed in, say, *The Colossus*
  by Sylvia Plath,
Is no different from an empty pair of dance shoes

Even if those shoes are in the middle of the Stardust Ballroom
With all the lights on, and hot music shakes the windows
  up and down the block.

This is the secret of inertia:
The shoes run on their own sense of the world.
They are in sympathy with the rock the kid skips
  over the lake
After it settles to the mud.
Not with the ripples,
But with the rock.

A practical and personal application of inertia
Can be found in the question:
Whose Turn Is It
To Take Out The Garbage?
An empty pair of dance shoes
Is a lot like the answer to this question,
As well as book-length poems
Set in the Midwest.

To sum up:
An empty pair of dance shoes
Is a lot like the sand the 98-pound weakling
  brushes from his cheeks
As the bully tows away his girlfriend.
Later,

When he spies the coupon at the back of the comic book,
He is about to act upon a different set of scientific principles.
He is ready to dance.

WALLFLOWERS

Maybe they alert what's left of our animal senses.
Perhaps this is why
They arouse such an equal mix
Of pity and relief
When they walk into a room.

They inhabit the defeat that surfaces in dreams,
The powerless dreams in which our cars take us
  like crazed, possessive lovers,
Or the classrooms where we become phantom teachers, our

Lesson plans become our character flaws in neon
  across the black sky of the board.
It is the only thing the students can read.

So we watch the way we dress
And are careful about the friends we think we choose,
And when we almost stop at their seats,
It is their eyes that keep us walking,
Because deep down, neither of us can explain how
  misfortune works, what makes

It stick, what causes both of us
  to sweat as if cornered.

JAZZ DANCER

I have a theory about motion.
I have a theory about the air.
I have a theory about main arteries and bass lines.
I have a theory about Friday night,
Just a theory, mind you,
About a dry mouth and certain kinds of thirst
And a once-a-month bulge of money
  in a working pair of pants.

I have a theory about kisses,
The way a woman draws a man across a dance floor
Like a ship approaching a new world.
I have a theory about space
And what's between the space

And an idea about words,
A theory about balance and the alphabet,
A theory concerning electricity and the tendons,
A hunch about long glances from across a ballroom
Even though there's a man on her arm,
Even though there's a woman on his arm

And Fire and the Ocean,
Stars and Earthquakes,
Explosions as sharp as new clothes
  off the rack.
When I leap,

Brushes strike the lip of a cymbal.
When I leap,
A note cuts through glass.
When I leap,

A thick finger dreams on a bass string
And all that sweat,
All that spittle,
All those cigarettes and cheap liquor,

All that lighthearted sass and volcanism,
All that volatile lipstick,
All that

Cleaves the air the way a man and woman
Sweet-talk in a bed.
When I leap,
I briefly see the world as it is
And as it should be

And the street where I grew up,
The saxophones,
Kisses
And mysteries among the houses

And my sister, dressing in front of her mirror,
A secret weapon of sound and motion,
A missionary
In the war against
The obvious.

THE WOMAN WHO DANCES WITH GOD

Let's assume that when we die
Our souls go to a heaven
That places a high premium
On aesthetic values.

Keeping this concept in mind,
How do we estimate our chances of getting in
Against this ballerina, who debuts a new dance,
Which I name
The Missionaries' Hop,
Right in front of the public television cameras?

Even if the angels placed a gun to my temple
I could never lift my bones like this.
If her theory is correct

She is on a date
With God.
God tosses her up
And she floats back as a handful of leaves.

I look at my young beer gut and worry.

If her theory is right,
Somewhere in a place she rises towards
A needle swings into the red zone
And a room is added to a house
I will be forbidden even to dream about.

THE BALLET CALLED JOHN THE BAPTIST

A man, walking down some street at dusk,
Spies a woman dancing for coins.
He stops to watch from a distance.
The woman struts like a rooster.
She tosses her head back and howls like a cat.

He moves closer.
The sun catches the faces of the observers:
Everyone
Is dressed in tatters.
Everyone stoops
As if born in a small room.
The woman steams like a Thanksgiving dinner.
One man beats time with a stick on a junked car,
Another wipes away tears
  with a caked and cynical hand.

They forget everything as the city goes on about its business,
As they circle each other.
Beside himself,
The man leaps into the center of the ring
And begins to dance.
He shakes as if he had just been dipped in a
  cold river
And he laughs; the woman laughs,
The men in the circle laugh

Until they no longer fit in the world.

CROWS IN A STRONG WIND

Off go the crows from the roof.
The crows can't hold on.
They might as well
Be perched on an oil slick.

Such an awkward dance,
These gentlemen
In their spottled-black coats.
Such a tipsy dance,

As if they didn't know where they were.
Such a humorous dance,
As they try to set things right,
As the wind reduces them.

Such a sorrowful dance.
How embarrassing is love
When it goes wrong

In front of everyone.

SEDUCTION

I am never alone in this world.
Here are the famous silhouettes on the
  window shade
And the reason they embrace:

The romantic ballad on the record player
That spills out of the window
Cracked a third of the way open

And down the block, where everyone else is dreaming
  or trying to dream,
Off the walls of the Baptist church,
Off the man who leans on the pharmacy at the corner
  waiting for the phone to ring,
Off the empty seats of the ice-cream parlor,

Around the corner to the all-night grocery
Where the kid behind the bullet-proof glass
  sways his hips,
His feet making tiny, absent steps
  upon the floorboards.

It is a spring night, and perhaps every street
  is like this,
The air rich and edible as fruit.
A couple, returning from a dance,
Takes the center of the sidewalk with a generous,
  uneven gait,
Aiming for each other's lips, but hitting the eyebrows,
  the forehead...

It doesn't matter. Tonight, as I watch from above
We all fall in love,
As would anyone who crosses the lovers' path
As their shadows glide across the front porches,
Brushing against the stoops,
Too busy to notice they're locked in the beat
Or that a light goes out above their heads.

DANCE AT THE AMHERST COUNTY PUBLIC LIBRARY

Fellow poets,
My Brothers and Sisters,
Comrades,
Distinguished guests and visitors,
Yes,
Even the tourists
In their T-shirts and mirrored sunglasses.

Before our attention begins to wander
Let me ask this:
In one hundred years,
No,
Say fifty years,
If, through grand design or fluke
The world still stands
And leads our descendants to this branch library in Amherst, VA,

Which poets would they find on the shelves?

The answer probably is
They will only find
What I found this afternoon:
Shakespeare
And Paul Laurence Dunbar.

In view of
And in spite of this awful truth,
I would still like to leave one or two thoughts behind:
If you are an archaeologist and find these items in Mr. Dunbar's
Collected Works:
This poem,
A pair of red laces

Please understand that this was how I defined myself,
A dancing fool who couldn't stay away from words
Even though they brought me nothing but difficulties.
I was better when I danced,
The language of the body so much cleaner.

I was always in jealous awe of the dancers,
Who seemed, to me at least, to be honest animals.
When I danced

I imagined myself a woman,
Because there is no sight more lovely
Than a woman kicking her heels up in a dive.

This is how I wasted my time,
Trying to become the Henry Ford of poetry,
And mass produce a group of words
Into a thing which could shake
And be owned by the entire world.

Naturally, I failed.

Of course, even the failure was a sort of dance.

My friend,
I bequeath to you what I know:
Not the image of a high, glistening city
But the potential in tall grass, flattened
  by a summer's storm.
Not the dance
But the good intentions of a dance.

This was the world I belonged to,
With its symphony of near-misses,
And in its name
And in the names of all those omitted
I dance my small graffiti dance.

2/1/08

811 Eady, Cornelius
Ead Victims of the Latest Dance Craze

	DATE DUE		
MAR 0 1 2008			
AUG 0 4 2010			

WITHDRAWN

Wellfleet Public Library
55 West Main Street
Wellfleet, MA 02667
508-349-0310
www.wellfleetlibrary.org